chocolate without borders

D1494718

chocolate without borders

JEAN-PIERRE WYBAUW

PHOTOGRAPHY FRANK CROES

 lannoo

Introducing the author

JEAN-PIERRE WYBAUW is a master chocolatier who is passionate about his profession. In the world of chocolate and confectionery he has a global reputation, because as technical advisor and demonstrator for the chocolate manufacturer Callebaut he has the task of passing on his knowledge to professionals in the trade. He is in constant demand, travelling round the world to give courses and lectures on chocolate in the most eminent professional training colleges in the United States, Canada, Japan, Australia and Germany. Jean-Pierre Wybauw holds several distinctions and prizes. In 2002 he was awarded the prestigious title of 'Chef of the Year' by the Culinary Institute of America. He is also in demand as a member of the jury in international competitions.

Foreword

For a long time I have dreamt of making a special book for chocoholics, housewives or new-age men.

With the aid of this book I want to explain in a straightforward and understandable way how to work with chocolate.

For many people it is, for example, always a mystery why this product sometimes has a beautiful gloss and sometimes not.

In an almost playful way this book shows how to turn chocolate easily out of moulds, how to make professional-looking chocolates, and how to make all kinds of delicious sweets and desserts with chocolate.

No specialized equipment is really necessary for this, although a food processor is a help, and the work is even easier if you have a small blender available. And another thing: the suggested oven temperatures and cooking times given are only guidelines and may vary from oven to oven.

Enjoy your chocolate experience!

JEAN-PIERRE WYBAUW

Contents

01 techniques

How to give a good gloss to chocolate

You often hear it said how difficult it is to give chocolate a beautiful gloss and make it properly hard once it has been melted. Nothing is less true, you just need to know what happens to the chocolate while it is being processed.

The main ingredient of chocolate is cocoa butter. If you look at hard chocolate under a microscope, you will see a picture full of cocoa butter crystals that fit neatly together. Because they are so beautifully arranged, the chocolate is shiny and hard, just like the chocolate that comes from a chocolate factory.

If you want to use chocolate to make something, it must, of course, first be melted. This makes all these beautifully arranged fat crystals melt away and the cocoa butter in the chocolate becomes liquid. If you let this melted chocolate cool again, then it usually becomes grey, looks grainy and stays quite soft.

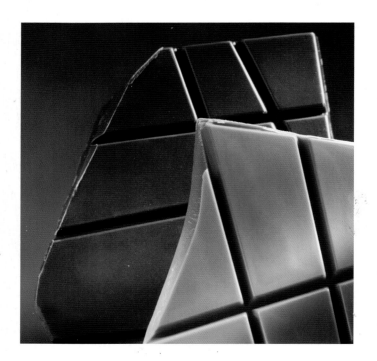

HOW CAN YOU ACHIEVE A GOOD RESULT?

The experts use the term 'tempering the chocolate' for this treatment, or 'precrystallization'. Many people wrongly think that the chocolate must be brought to a specific temperature for this. But the crux of the matter is to try and get the cocoa butter crystals back, and for this a thermometer is very little use.

To understand this better, you could compare it with butter, because it coagulates in more or less the same way as chocolate. Obviously you can't replace the cocoa butter by butter, but the crystallization process is very similar. If the chocolate becomes nicely hard and glossy, this is, as it is with butter, due to the way the fat has been correctly crystallized out. The fat in the chocolate is the cocoa butter.

THE COMPARISON BELOW EXPLAINS WHAT HAPPENS IN EACH CASE:

BUTTER	CHOCOLATE
Good, fresh butter gives a pleasant, soft feeling as it melts in the mouth, because it consists of small, slowly melting fat crystals.	Chocolate also gives a pleasant and gently melting sensation in the mouth, because it consists of microscopic, fine fat crystals.

Melting

Butter turns to oil. (All the fat crystals have melted away.)	Chocolate becomes liquid. (Usually all the crystals have melted.)

Re-coagulation

The oil turns into a grainy and unattractive butter. Taste and appearance are unpleasant. (There are now large and irregular fat crystals.)	Idem. The chocolate turns grey and grainy. The gloss is lacking and it melts very quickly when touched. (There are now large, irregular fat crystals.)

THERE ARE THREE POSSIBLE WAYS OF GIVING BUTTER ITS BEAUTIFUL SMOOTH AND CREAMY STRUCTURE BACK AGAIN.

- Melt only two-thirds of it. The remaining third still contains enough crystals to influence the two-thirds of oil.
- Stir it while cooling it until it gets slightly thicker. This takes a long time.
- Add bits of butter to the oil until you get a light thickening.

THE PRECRYSTALLIZATION OF CHOCOLATE

The simplest way is to melt two-thirds of the chocolate, and chop up one third of it reasonably fine. In the melted part all the crystals have melted away, while the finely chopped chocolate is still full of good crystals which we absolutely need for the gloss, the hardness and the contractile strength of the final product. So you will have to add crystals, and these are all to be found in the hard and finely chopped chocolate. The best way is just to stir a little of this chopped chocolate through the melted part.

- If the pieces of chocolate melt away easily, this means that the chocolate is still too hot. In that case add a little at a time until after stirring a little more you notice that they no longer melt away, or only with difficulty.
- If the pieces no longer melt away, this means that too many pieces (crystals) have been added. You can't get any beautiful results in this way and it will be difficult to work with, because this chocolate will thicken too quickly. In that case, carefully heat it a little to make the last undissolved pieces disappear. But take care, because if the temperature gets too high, the crystals melt away and so fresh pieces of chocolate will again have to be added.

TESTING

How can you be sure that the chocolate is ready to eat? In other words, how do you know whether the proper crystals are there? Dip the point of a knife in the chocolate, and put it to one side for a moment. Or put a small quantity, a few drops is enough, on a piece of greaseproof paper. If the chocolate begins to set within a few minutes it has been precrystallized. And then at last you can go to work and do nice things with that chocolate. Another thing: if while you are working the chocolate begins to thicken slightly, this means that too many crystals are beginning to form again, and you should carefully raise the temperature, as described above. In this way you can if necessary keep the chocolate in good condition for hours.

Chocolate in moulds

YOU CAN MAKE ALL KINDS OF FIGURES AND SHAPES WITH CHOCOLATE. THE TIPS BELOW SHOULD CERTAINLY HELP YOU TO SUCCEED.

- The moulds should be conical.
- To be able to make a nice, glossy chocolate figure the mould too should have a glossy shine.
- Plastic moulds are ideal. The plastic should, of course, be suitable for foodstuffs.
- Glass moulds are not suitable.
- The moulds must be spotlessly clean. The slightest spot or fingerprint will show up on the chocolate.

USE YOUR IMAGINATION AND LOOK AROUND YOU. THERE ARE MASSES OF MOULDS THAT YOU CAN USE:

- Moulds made for ice cubes are also suitable for making chocolates.
- In the stores you'll find plastic eggs, Christmas trees, Father Christmases, and so on, filled with sweets. Take them apart and for each one you will have two moulds.
- The conical bases of some small or larger mineral water bottles. These will serve to make small tubs that can afterwards be filled with puddings.
- Scallop shells, lined with kitchen foil.

POURING LIQUID CHOCOLATE INTO MOULDS

Preferably work with chocolate which has a high cocoa butter content. Callebaut's 'Callets' are ideal for this (p.32, Dipping Chocolates).

Always work with precrystallized chocolate.

Pour the mould full of chocolate and make sure that it is all well covered. Shake the mould a little to prevent any air bubbles forming in the chocolate figure. Turn the mould upside down, so that any excess chocolate can run back into its container. Place the mould on a rack or on greaseproof paper to let it harden. As soon as the chocolate no longer sticks, cut away any unwanted edges with a knife.

Place the mould in the refrigerator for at least 20 minutes to give the chocolate time to shrink and to come away from the side of the mould.

Turn it out on a clean work surface.

For shapes that need to be fixed together, such as Easter eggs, heat a baking tray very slightly. Press both shapes quickly on the hot tray so that the edges melt slightly, and immediately stick both halves together.

With scallop shells, first moisten the shell a little so that the kitchen foil sticks to it better. Use your fingers or a brush to smooth the chocolate on the mould.

After it has hardened, brush on another layer to get a sufficiently thick shell, or the chocolate will break when you turn it out.

It is important to know that the layer of chocolate must be thick enough, because too thin a layer will not come out of the mould. Then the chocolate has not enough strength to loosen itself from the mould.

And finally: the thickness of the shell also depends on the size of the mould. The larger the mould, the thicker the shell must be. So for larger shapes you will need to pour the chocolate twice to get a sufficiently thick shell.

Amusing chocolate shapes

Requirements

chocolate

mixing bowl

spatula

spoon

greaseproof paper or

aluminium foil

pastry or marzipan cutters

A large variety of cutters is available from kitchenware departments in stores.

METHOD 1

Take a flat baking sheet and cover it with greaseproof paper. Pour chocolate on this and smooth it to an even thickness with a palette knife.

Move the sheet about a little to remove any air bubbles from the chocolate.

As soon as the chocolate has set and doesn't stick any more, use the cutters to cut out fancy shapes from the chocolate.

To avoid the chocolate curling up while it hardens, turn the sheet with the chocolate upside down as fast as possible.

METHOD 2

Place the cutters on a baking sheet covered with paper or aluminium foil.

Precrystallize the chocolate. Use a spoon to pour chocolate into the cutters to the desired thickness. Move the baking sheet carefully back and forth so that the chocolate will flow smoothly.

Put it in the refrigerator for at least 20 minutes to harden.

Carefully remove the shapes from the moulds.

As a finishing touch you can decorate the motifs with chocolate or with a glaze of egg white.

An egg-white glaze consists of icing sugar mixed with egg white. Add icing sugar to an egg white until you have a fairly thick mixture. Stir well to make it a little lighter. Add a little more sugar if it is still too liquid. The glaze should be easy to use in a piping bag. You can add a few drops of lemon juice to the glaze to make it dry out faster.

Quick and easy ways of making cake decorations

CUTTING OUT SHAPES

Precrystallize the chocolate.

Pour a small quantity on a sheet of greaseproof paper. For a high gloss, put the chocolate on plastic or cellophane. Immediately brush the chocolate out evenly. Allow the chocolate to harden a little until it is no longer sticky. Cut all the shapes out with the point of a sharp knife, or make use of cutters. These are available from stores selling confectioners' provisions and also in ordinary supermarkets.

The most convenient method is to make a drawing on card beforehand and cut it out, so that you have a template to help you to cut the chocolate to shape. Immediately after cutting it out, the whole sheet of chocolate must be turned over to let it harden, otherwise the chocolate will curl upwards.

If you use shiny foil, it is necessary to leave the foil on the chocolate for half an hour before you take it away, so that the high gloss will stay on the chocolate.

LEAVES

Holly: wash the holly leaves and leave them to dry. With the help of a brush or finger, spread the chocolate over the leaves. The layer of chocolate should be thick enough to allow it to come away from the leaf.

Let it harden well before removing the leaf from the chocolate.

Plastic flowers: remove the petals from the flowers, wash and dry them. Then proceed as described above.

FANCIFUL SHAPES

Scatter some granulated sugar on a plate.

Make a drawing in the sugar with your finger or with a stick.

Fill a paper piping bag (see page 27) with chocolate and pipe in the drawing. Let it harden properly before removing it.

A variant: use cocoa instead of sugar.

There are two methods:

- Spread precrystallized chocolate thinly on a piece of marble. Spread backwards and forwards a few times until it no longer sticks. With a triangular knife (a filling knife) at an angle of 45 degrees quickly scrape the chocolate from the marble surface.
- Directly from a chocolate bar:
  Put the bar of chocolate on the table with the flat side upwards. Put a plate with a rim against it.
  With the help of a large knife, scrape flakes from the block. For this hold the handle of the knife in one hand and with the other hand press on the point of the knife. This method does demand some practice, but you will get your flakes more quickly and it is less messy.

CURLS

Take a bar of chocolate and let it stand in a warm place for a few hours, so that the chocolate gets a little softer. Take a parer and pare curls off the side of the bar with it.

Pull the side of a bar of chocolate across a grater
Ideal for scattering over a cake or to roll truffles in.

WITH A PAPER PIPING BAG

- Take some cling film. Pipe parallel lines quite
  close to each other. Then pipe similar lines at
  right angles to them. Leave this to harden.
  You can break this grid into pieces or cut it with a
  hot cutter or knife.
- Shapes
  Draw the outlines of various shapes on paper.
  Put a piece of kitchen foil quite flat on this. Pipe
  chocolate along the lines. Let it harden a little.
  To prevent the chocolate curling upwards, turn the
  shape upside down before the chocolate has
  completely hardened.

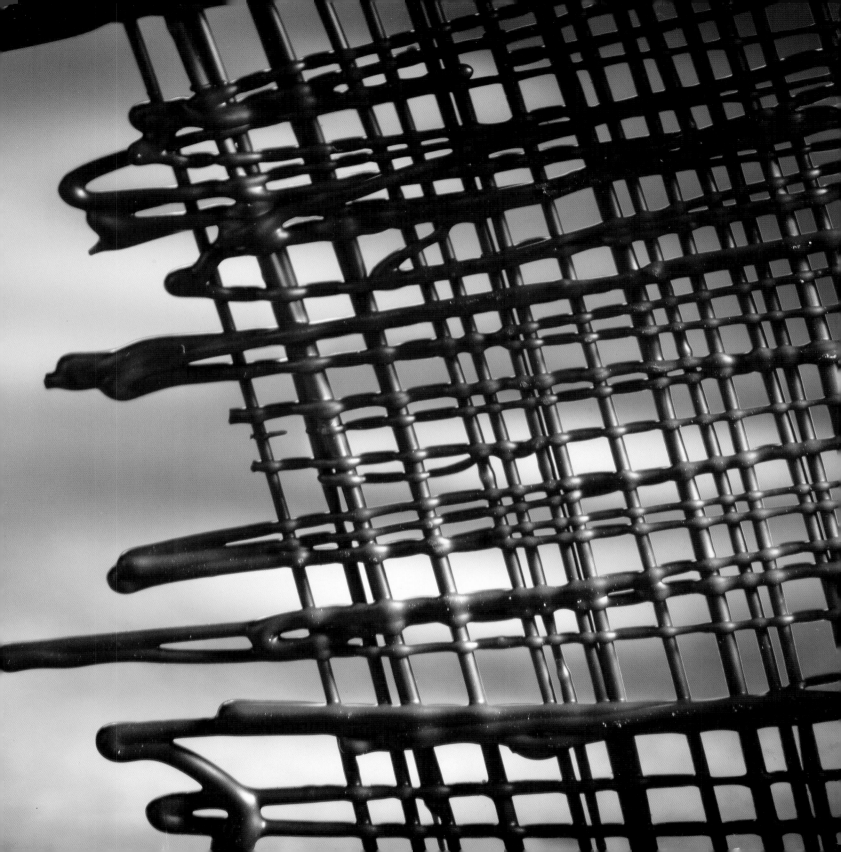

  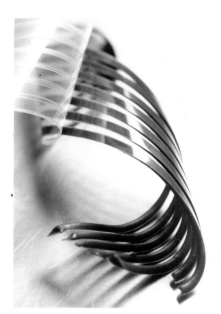 

CHOCOLATE SPIRALS

Cut a piece of plastic film about 3 x 15 cm. The transparent files in which documents are kept are perfect for this. Spread the melted chocolate very thinly on this. With the help of a plastic comb (you can get them in supermarkets) cut long, fine channels through the chocolate. Leave the chocolate to thicken slightly before you shape it into a spiral.

Place the spiral in the refrigerator for at least 10 minutes and then remove the plastic film.

Making a paper piping bag for decorations

Cut a square sheet of greaseproof paper across diagonally, so that you have two triangles.

Place your thumb and index finger two cm above the middle of the long side and fold the longer part over your fingers and the shorter part the other way.

Roll the paper up into a cone and with your thumb and index finger draw it out to a point. Fold the corners at the top of the cone so that the paper does not lose its shape.

Hold the bag at a slant while you fill it with chocolate. Only fill it two-thirds full, then you can still easily close the top by folding down the top point of the bag tightly.

Now fold both sides inwards and finally fold down the top again.

To get the piping thickness you want, cut off part of the point.

When decorating, press on the top and hold the folded parts tight, so that no chocolate comes out of it.

Take care: don't fill the bag too full; it will make it more difficult to pipe with it.

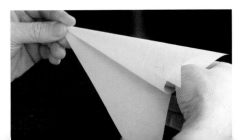

Light and crispy clusters
Crisp chocolate bars
Dipping chocolates
Orangettes
Kirsch truffles
Chocolate truffles
Cream truffles with cinnamon
Chocolates with Cointreau cream centres
Marzipan chocolates
Chocolates with an orange peel and hazelnut centre
Fudge chocolates
Chocolates with fruit centres
Soft chocolate caramels
Baked marzipan
Muesli squares

02 chocolate confectionery

Light and crispy clusters

Requirements

chocolate
Rice Krispies
mixing bowl
spatula
small ice-cream scoop or a
teaspoon
greaseproof paper, non-
stick baking foil or plain
aluminium foil

METHOD OF PREPARATION

Put a quantity of Rice Krispies in a mixing bowl.

Pour some precrystallized chocolate over it.

Mix it in quickly until all the Rice Krispies are covered. To get light and crispy clusters, add as little chocolate as possible. It is not possible to give precise quantities, because the result depends on the kind of chocolate used and personal taste.

Using the ice-cream scoop, heap small clusters on paper, or take a little of the mixture in the bowl with a teaspoon and push it off the spoon with your finger. Leave them to harden completely and then take them off the paper.

To preserve the chocolate aroma, keep the clusters in a closed biscuit tin.

VARIANT

Replace the Rice Krispies with chopped and roasted nuts, raisins or a mixture of both. In that case you can't, of course, call them 'light' any more.

Crisp chocolate bars

Requirements

chocolate
cornflakes, finely chopped
and roasted nuts or roasted
sesame seeds
piping bag
greaseproof paper or alu-
minium foil

Ideal as decoration on ice-cream coupes,
or simply as a tea-time treat.

METHOD OF PREPARATION
Precrystallize the chocolate.
Fill a piping bag with it. Quickly pipe long,
thick lines on the paper. At once, and
while the chocolate is still liquid, scatter
the finely chopped nuts or sesame seeds
generously over them.

If you are using cornflakes, it is better to break them
into smaller pieces first.
Leave the chocolate to set and cut the lines into bars of
the desired length.

Dipping chocolates

A FEW USEFUL TIPS ON DIPPING CHOCOLATES

The chocolate must, of course, be precrystallized (see p. 14 - 15). To get the best gloss, the chocolates should be at room temperature before they are dipped in the liquid chocolate. After they have been dipped, the chocolates should not be put in the refrigerator straightaway.

To get a good result, it is sensible to buy chocolate with a high enough cocoa-butter content. In the trade 'couverture' is used: that is chocolate with a higher cocoa-butter content than chocolate bars. You can only find this couverture in special shops or from dealers in confectionery ingredients. In supermarkets it is also available, for instance in the form of

Callebaut's 'Callets', in 500 g packets. The same Callets are sold in the trade, but then in 2.5 kg packs.

Chocolate bars are not suitable for dipping, because they produce too thick a liquid and so form a very thick layer of chocolate cover round the centres.

Dipping is best done with a dipping fork. This is a fork with thin tines, developed specially for this work. The finished product slides easily off the fork, leaving no ugly marks or drips. They are available from firms selling confectionery equipment and are not expensive. If you can't obtain a dipping fork, you can try an ordinary table fork, or even a cocktail stick. There are also very good melting pans, specially designed for this purpose. They are very reasonably priced. First you set the thermostat to 'melt' and then turn it back a little to lower the temperature. Now the chocolate must be carefully precrystallized (as described on p.12: 'How to give a good gloss to chocolate'). The advantage is that you can go on working with the chocolate for hours before it starts to cool down. For the melting pans see www.moldart.be. Take care that there is enough chocolate in the pan, so that the centres can be dipped deep enough for them to be completely covered.

Use the fork to lift the finished product up and then tap the fork a few times on the edge of the pan, so that any excess chocolate runs off back into the pan.

Let the dipped chocolate slide off the fork onto greaseproof paper or a piece of aluminium foil. You can add a decoration by placing the fork on top of coating while it is still liquid and carefully lifting it. Then leave the finished chocolates to harden, without putting them in the refrigerator.

Orangettes

Requirements

To make about 500 g finished orangettes

200 g candied orange peel in
strips
icing sugar
at least 300 g chocolate
fork or sugar tongs
greaseproof paper or
aluminium foil

METHOD OF PREPARATION

Separate the pieces of peel and put them to dry on a rack for half a day.
Scatter a little icing sugar over them and rub it into them, so that they become less
sticky.
Melt the chocolate and precrystallize it.
Dip the strips one by one into the chocolate with the aid of a fork or sugar tongs,
and put them on the greaseproof paper.
Allow them to harden well.

Kirsch truffles

Requirements

To make about 75 truffles

150 g cream
100 g Kirsch
40 g butter
450 g chocolate
piping bag
greaseproof paper

METHOD OF PREPARATION

Bring the butter to room temperature.

Melt the chocolate in a bain marie.

Bring the cream to the boil and pour it over the chocolate.

Stir the soft butter into the chocolate cream.

Finally add the Kirsch and stir it all until you have a nice, smooth batter.

Leave it all to thicken slightly until you have a mixture that can be piped.

With the aid of a piping bag with a smooth nozzle of about 8 mm diameter, pipe small balls onto greaseproof paper.

Leave them to set in the refrigerator.

Finish the truffles by dipping the balls one after the other into precrystallized chocolate and then rolling them through chocolate flakes. Leave long enough to set, and then remove any surplus flakes.

Chocolate truffles

Requirements

150 g chocolate
100 g butter
2 egg yolks
50 g cream
50 g sugar
vanilla essence
cocoa
piping bag or small ice-
cream scoop

To make about 60 truffles

METHOD OF PREPARATION

Melt the chocolate and add first the melted butter, then the egg yolks and the vanilla. Bring the cream and the sugar to the boil and pour it onto the chocolate mixture. Stir until you have a homogeneous mixture.

Leave this to cool in the refrigerator until it begins to show signs of setting along the edge of the bowl.

Use a piping bag with a smooth nozzle to pipe small balls on greaseproof paper.

Or use a small ice-cream scoop to shape small balls.

Place them in the refrigerator for 10 minutes.

Meanwhile precrystallize the dipping chocolate.

Dip the balls one by one in the chocolate and put them on the cocoa. Using two forks, roll the dipped truffles through the cocoa.

Leave them to harden. Remove the surplus cocoa and serve the truffles on a dish.

Cream truffles with cinnamon

Requirements

200 g icing sugar
350 g chocolate
200 g cream
100 g ground cinnamon
piping bag

To make about 80 truffles

GARNISH

Mix 200 g icing sugar with 100 g ground cinnamon.

METHOD OF PREPARATION

Chop the chocolate finely.
Bring the cream to the boil with the cinnamon, and pour it onto the chocolate.
Stir well until you have a homogeneous mixture.
Leave to cool a little in the refrigerator, until the mixture starts to set on the edge of the bowl. Whip the mixture lightly.
Immediately pipe oval shapes onto greaseproof paper, using a piping bag with a smooth nozzle. Place the piped truffles in the refrigerator for 30 minutes.
Meanwhile precrystallize some chocolate for dipping.
Dip the truffles one by one in the chocolate and roll them straightaway through the garnish.
When the chocolate has hardened completely, remove any surplus powder.
Serve them on a pretty plate.

Chocolates with Cointreau cream centres

Requirements

To make about 40 chocolates

150 g cream
60 g butter
250 g milk chocolate or
white chocolate
15 g Cointreau liqueur
piping bag
palette knife
greaseproof paper
chocolate mould, or if this is
not available, a mould for
making ice cubes

TO PREPARE THE FILLING

Chop the chocolate finely. Bring the cream to the boil.
While stirring continuously, pour the boiled cream onto the finely chopped chocolate.
Add the liqueur and finally the butter which should be at room temperature.

TO PREPARE THE CHOCOLATE SHELLS

Precrystallize the chocolate. Using a small ladle, pour the chocolate over the moulds and keep the moulds slightly tilted while doing this, so that the surplus chocolate flows back into the bowl. Scrape the surplus chocolate from the surface and the sides. Shake the mould a few times from side to side to remove any air pockets from the chocolate, as these will create small holes in the shell of the finished product and that would not look attractive. Turn the mould over at once to remove the surplus chocolate and to retain a certain thickness of the shell. Next put the mould on greaseproof paper with the open side down. Take care: if the shell is too thin, the chocolate will not come out of the mould and will break. As soon as the chocolate no longer sticks to the paper, turn the mould round again and scrape the surface smooth. With a piping bag you can now pipe the cooled cream filling into the moulded shells. Make sure that the cream filling stays 2 mm below the edge of the chocolate shells. Too much cream in the mould will stop you making a neat finish to the chocolates later on. If by accident too much cream has been piped in, then you should remove the excess straight away. Let the cream set properly before closing the shells.
Close off the filled shells with a minimal quantity of chocolate, using a palette knife. Smooth the surface carefully as you work. The mould should now be placed in the refrigerator for at least 30 minutes.
Put a sheet of greaseproof paper on the table. Turn the moulds quickly upside-down on the paper. If the chocolates don't come away easily, give a gentle tap to the mould with the blunt edge of a knife. Keep the chocolates in a tin.

Marzipan chocolates

Requirements

To make about 40 chocolates

125 g ground almonds
125 g icing sugar
60 g grenadine or
rosewater
chocolate for dipping
greaseproof paper
food processor

TO PREPARE THE MARZIPAN

Mix the ground almonds with the icing sugar in the food processor. It is essential to add a little grenadine or rosewater to moisten the mixture, otherwise oil will be released by the almonds and this will result in a greasy and unappealing marzipan. If you add too much moisture, the resulting marzipan will be very tasty, but feel limp and sticky, so that it is difficult to work with. If this happens you can later add a little powdered sugar to it. Instead of grenadine or rosewater, other flavours can be added, but it is essential that enough moisture is added. Let the food processor turn until the marzipan starts to clump together. A Magimix food processor is ideal for this kind of work, because it has three different sizes of mixing bowls, to suit the size and consistency of the mixture you want to produce in it.

TO MAKE THE CHOCOLATES

Roll out the marzipan to an even thickness, using a rolling pin. The surface on which you roll out the marzipan should be dusted with icing sugar to avoid the marzipan sticking to it. Scatter some icing sugar over the top too. With a knife, divide the marzipan into equal cubes and leave them to rest for at least an hour before covering them with chocolate. If you don't do this, then the chocolates may later on show cracks, because of the after-effects of the marzipan. Precrystallize the chocolate. Push a cocktail stick into a cube of marzipan and dip it completely into the liquid chocolate. Hold a fork in the other hand. Gently put the cube on greaseproof paper and remove the stick at once by pushing against the surface of the chocolate with the fork. This fork impression at the same time provides the finished product with a decoration. In the trade use is made of a dipping fork which is produced in various shapes. There are forks with two, three, four or more tines. To avoid making ugly marks on the bottom of the chocolates, these tines are very fine.

Chocolates with orange peel and hazelnut centres

Requirements

To make about 65 filled chocolates

250 g plain chocolate
1 egg yolk
100 g icing sugar
40 g whipping cream
40 g rum
150 g hazelnuts, roasted and roughly chopped
75 g candied orange peel, finely chopped
greaseproof paper

METHOD OF PREPARATION

Melt the chocolate.

Stir the egg yolk well with the sugar, and add the cream and the rum to it.

Add this mixture to the chocolate and mix it all to a smooth batter.

Mix in the hazelnut and candied peel. Leave to rest for 10 minutes.

Dust the work surface with some icing sugar to avoid the mixture sticking to it; scatter some on the mixture, too, and roll this out with a rolling pin to a thickness of 1 cm. Use a round or square cutter to cut out shapes or cut squares from the slab with a knife.

Leave to rest for 1 hour.

TO FINISH

Meanwhile precrystallize the chocolate for dipping.

Use a fork to dip the pieces of filling in the chocolate.

Let it harden on greaseproof paper or aluminium paper.

If you like, you can add a little decoration.

Fudge chocolates

Requirements

150 g sugar
100 g demerara sugar
100 g milk
60 g chocolate, finely
chopped
30 g butter
a little vanilla essence
greaseproof paper or
aluminium foil
non-stick baking sheet
if possible a thermometer
showing temperatures above
100 °C

To make about 40 chocolates

METHOD OF PREPARATION

Bring the milk to the boil together with the sugars. Add the finely chopped chocolate, then the butter and the vanilla essence, and continue to cook to 112 °C–115 °C. Stop stirring as soon as the mixture reaches boiling point, otherwise the syrup will run to sugar too early. In the trade a thermometer is used which shows temperatures above 100 °C. You can manage without this thermometer by boiling the syrup until it begins to thicken slightly, and occasionally testing by dipping a spoonful of syrup in cold water and waiting until the syrup is completely cold. You should then be able to form it into a small ball.

Let the mixture get lukewarm. Meanwhile butter a baking tray or use a non-stick baking sheet. Stir the mixture until it begins to crystallize slightly. Pour it onto the tray or sheet, and immediately spread it evenly to about 1 to 1.5 cm. Leave to cool completely before cutting it into small cubes. Dip these cubes in precrystallized chocolate and leave them to set on greaseproof paper or aluminium foil.

Chocolates with fruit centres

Requirements

250 g apricot pulp
(for instance, tinned)
250 g sugar
blender
greaseproof paper or
aluminium foil

To make about 35 chocolates

TO PREPARE

Allow the apricot pulp to simmer on a low heat for about 10 minutes. Grease a rimmed baking tray with oil. Pulp the softened apricots in a blender.

Add the sugar and continue simmering on a low heat until the mixture has thickened considerably.

Test a small spoonful of the mixture by letting it cool completely and then feel between thumb and index finger whether the fruit mixture is firm enough. Professionals use a special thermometer for this. They boil the pulp with the sugar to 107 °C. If the mixture is too soft, it should be left to boil a little longer. Take care to leave it on a low heat and keep stirring to avoid burning. Pour the boiling mixture onto the oiled tray and leave it to cool down completely. Cut it into the required size. Precrystallize the dipping chocolate. To get a firm base and to make it easier to get the confection out of the dipping chocolate with a fork, spread a thin layer of chocolate over the surface of each cube with your finger. When the chocolate has hardened, turn each centre over.

With a fork, dip each fruit centre into the chocolate and place it on greaseproof paper or aluminium foil. To decorate, push the flat side of the fork gently onto the still wet surface to draw a few lines.

VARIANT

Roll the cubes through granulated sugar instead of dipping them in chocolate.

Soft chocolate caramels

Requirements

200 g cream
250 g sugar
a pinch of salt
100 g acacia honey
10 g butter
200 g dark chocolate

To make about 80 caramels

METHOD OF PREPARATION

Bring the cream to the boil together with the sugar and the salt. Let it boil well for a few minutes. Add the honey, butter and chopped chocolate and continue boiling at 120 °C. If you have no thermometer available, put a small bowl of very cold water ready for testing. As soon as the caramel syrup begins to thicken, take a small quantity on a wooden spoon and let this drop into the cold water. Wait a moment until the caramel has gone completely cold, and then feel how firm it is. It should be just possible to knead it into a small, malleable ball that does not cling to your teeth when you bite it. Pour the mixture into a rimmed, buttered baking tray. Leave it to cool down completely. Cut the slab of caramel with a sawing movement into squares of the required size. Put the caramels at once in a well-closed tin or cover each caramel with chocolate.

Baked marzipan

Scatter some icing sugar on your work surface to avoid the slabs of marzipan sticking to the surface.

Lightly knead the marzipan to a smooth mass.

Use a rolling pin to roll out the marzipan evenly. Scatter a little icing sugar over the top of the marzipan.

With a knife cut regular squares or rectangles, or use cutters in decorative shapes.

Place the marzipan shapes on a non-stick baking tray or use an ordinary buttered baking tray.

Bake in a preheated oven at 180 °C, until the edges begin to change colour.

To prevent the marzipan drying out, you can coat the top of the marzipan with a little egg white.

If desired, the marzipan can be partly dipped in chocolate by way of decoration, after it has cooled down.

Muesli squares

Requirements

chocolate
raisins
various nuts
mixing bowl
greaseproof paper
baking tray or flat dish
knife

METHOD OF PREPARATION

Mix all the nuts and raisins in a bowl.

Pour the carefully melted chocolate over it and mix it quickly.

Pour everything at once onto greaseproof paper on a tray, spread out the mixture to an even thickness with a knife.

Move the tray from side to side, so that the mixture spreads out to a nice smooth surface.

Work quickly, because the chocolate will set quite fast.

As soon as the chocolate no longer feels sticky, cut the slab into squares.

Make sure you don't wait too long, because when the chocolate has hardened, it can no longer be cut. In that case you should simply break it into irregular shapes – this has its own charm.

Viennese whirls
Crumbly muesli bars
Chocolate brownies
Chocolate butter biscuits
Chocolate volcanoes
Oatmeal and chocolate biscuits
Chocolate chip biscuits
Coconut mini cakes
Wafer-thin coffee tuiles
Almond-paste cake
Sponge biscuits

o3 biscuits

Viennese whirls

Requirements

To make about 20 biscuits

125 g butter
70 g icing sugar
20 g vanilla sugar
175 g plain flour
25 g cornflour
10 g baking powder
75 g dark chocolate
50 g milk
baking tray or non-stick mat
greaseproof paper

METHOD OF PREPARATION

Melt the chocolate.

Mix the butter with the sugars till light and airy.

Sift the flour together with the cornflour and the baking powder, and stir it into the butter and sugar.

Add the milk and finally the chocolate.

Preheat the oven to 170 °C.

Grease a baking tray with butter or use a non-stick baking mat.

Using a piping bag with a serrated nozzle, pipe whirls onto the baking tray with a zigzag movement.

Bake for 12 to 15 minutes.

TO FINISH

If desired, dip the biscuits halfway into precrystallized chocolate and leave them to harden on greaseproof paper.

Crumbly muesli bars

Requirements

150 g chocolate
90 g sugar
90 g demerara sugar
100 g hazelnuts
2 eggs
250 g plain flour
500 g butter
1 sachet baking powder
60 g Rice Krispies
chopper
greaseproof paper

To make about 22 pieces

METHOD OF PREPARATION

Butter a baking tray or use a non-stick baking mat.

Toast the hazelnuts.

When cooled, crush them in a chopper so fine that only a liquid paste remains.

If you haven't got a chopper you should be able to find pure hazelnut paste in health food shops.

Preheat the oven to 190 °C.

Finely chop the chocolate.

Soften the butter and stir the sugars, hazelnuts and eggs into it.

Mix well. Add the flour and the baking powder.

Finally stir in the chocolate pieces.

Scatter half of the Rice Krispies over the baking tray so that the bottom is covered.

Pour the batter onto the Rice Krispies and push it down well until you have a layer about 1.5 cm thick. Scatter the remaining Rice Krispies over the top.

Bake for 30 minutes.

Leave to cool. Divide into bars.

If desired, dip the bottom of the bars in chocolate and put the bars on greaseproof paper. Keep them in a closed tin.

Chocolate brownies

Requirements

To make about 20 portions

100 g plain flour
4 g baking powder
10 g cocoa
3 eggs
140 g sugar
a pinch of salt
90 g butter
60 g rum
300 g dark chocolate

METHOD OF PREPARATION

Sieve the flour together with the baking powder and the cocoa.

Melt the butter and mix it with the flour mixture together with the salt and the rum.

Beat the eggs with the sugar till light and airy and add them to the mixture.

Add the melted chocolate.

Pour the mixture into a buttered baking tin of about 20 x 20 cm.

Bake for 35 minutes at 180 °C.

Chocolate butter biscuits

Requirements

To make 50 biscuits

150 g butter
60 g sugar
180 g plain flour
60 g chocolate

METHOD OF PREPARATION

Melt the chocolate. Soften the butter in a bowl and mix it with the sugar.

Sift the flour and add it to the butter.

Finally add the melted chocolate and mix it to a homogeneous dough.

Leave to rest for 30 minutes in the refrigerator. Preheat the oven to 160 °C.

Meanwhile butter a baking tray or use a non-stick baking tray.

Roll out the dough on a lightly floured work surface to a thickness of about 1 cm.

Using a ruler, draw strips on the dough and cut them out with a knife. Divide these strips into rectangles of about 1.5 cm width and put them on the baking tray.

Bake them for about 30 minutes.

After baking leave them to cool on a rack.

Chocolate volcanoes

Requirements

To make 40 biscuits

200 g plain flour
80 g icing sugar
50 g chocolate
150 g butter
2 egg yolks
granulated sugar
1 egg yolk

METHOD OF PREPARATION

Melt the chocolate.

Sift the flour and the icing sugar.

Soften the butter and stir the flour mixture into it.

Add the two egg yolks one at a time and then the chocolate, and knead the whole to a smooth dough.

Allow the dough to harden in the refrigerator for 1 hour.

Roll the dough into cylinders, brush the outside with egg yolk and roll them in granulated sugar. Leave the dough to rest in the refrigerator for 1 hour.

Preheat the oven to 180 °C.

Cut round slices about 1 cm thick and place them on a buttered baking tray or on a non-stick baking mat.

Bake them for about 20 minutes.

When they have cooled down, keep them in a closed tin.

Oatmeal and chocolate biscuits

Requirements

To make 20 biscuits

125 g butter
175 g sugar
30 g vanilla sugar
125 g oatmeal
1 egg
100 g self-raising flour
50 g chocolate
saw-toothed knife

METHOD OF PREPARATION

Chop the chocolate roughly. Preheat the oven to 160 °C. Butter a baking tray or use a non-stick baking mat. Soften the butter and mix it with the sugars. Add the oatmeal, the flour and the egg to it and knead everything to a smooth dough. Finally work the pieces of chocolate into the dough. Shape the dough into a roll and leave this to stiffen in the refrigerator for 30 minutes. Using a saw-toothed knife, cut the roll into slices and put them 5 cm apart on the baking tray.
Bake them for 25 minutes until they have a nice brown colour.

Chocolate chip biscuits

Requirements

To make about 20 biscuits

125 g butter
90 g demerara sugar
50 g sugar
1 sachet vanilla sugar
1 egg
150 g chocolate
175 g plain flour
10 g baking powder
small ice-cream scoop or
tablespoon

METHOD OF PREPARATION

Preheat the oven to 190 °C. Butter two baking trays or make use of non-stick mats. Chop the chocolate into rough pieces. Mix the butter with the sugars. Add the egg, the baking powder and the flour, and mix well until you have a smooth dough. Finally mix the chocolate into it.

Put small piles of dough on the baking tray with the aid of a small ice-cream scoop or a tablespoon. Make sure that they are put well apart, because they spread considerably during baking. Bake the biscuits for 10 to 12 minutes until they are a pale golden brown.

Leave the biscuits to cool on a rack.

Coconut mini cakes

Requirements

250 g butter
180 g powdered sugar
80 g plain flour
7 egg whites
100 g grated coconut
180 g chocolate
piping bag
small cake moulds or non-stick
moulds

To make about 30 small cakes

METHOD OF PREPARATION

Preheat the oven to 220 °C. Butter the moulds or use non-stick moulds. Melt the chocolate. Mix the butter, which should be at room temperature, with the sugar and the flour to a homogeneous dough. Next add the grated coconut and the chocolate. Whisk the egg whites until they form peaks and carefully fold them into the mixture. Pipe the mixture into the moulds until they are about three-quarters full. Bake them for about 12 minutes.

Wafer-thin coffee tuiles

Requirements

To make about 10 tuiles

200 g finely chopped almonds

200 g powdered sugar

30 g plain flour

160 g butter

10 g finely ground coffee

50 g milk

METHOD OF PREPARATION

Melt the butter slightly. Mix the sugar with the flour and the chopped almonds.

Add the melted butter and the coffee. Finally add the milk.

Stir the mixture until quite smooth. Leave this to rest for about 1 hour in the refrigerator.

Roll small balls by hand (a small teaspoonful at the time) and put these on a non-stick

baking tray at least 10 cm apart. Press the small balls flat and make sure they keep a nicely

rounded shape.

Bake in an oven at 180 °C until they begin to colour slightly.

Leave them to cool. Keep them in a closed biscuit tin.

Almond-paste cake

Requirements

shortcrust pastry (see p.112)
marzipan
chocolate
egg yolk
pine kernels
piping bag
brush

METHOD OF PREPARATION

Roll out a sheet of shortcrust pastry thinly to a thickness of about 3 mm.

With the aid of a round, scalloped cutter of about 8 cm diameter, cut out rounds and put them on a baking tray. Leave them to rest a little.

Pipe a quantity of chocolate (about a tablespoonful) into the centre of each round. Leave the chocolate to harden a little.

Brush the rounds lightly with water.

Roll out a piece of marzipan thinly to about 3 cm thickness and use a scalloped cutter of about 6 cm diameter to cut out rounds. Moisten them slightly with water and stick them to the first circle (with the moistened side down). Make sure that the chocolate has been completely covered.

Brush them all over with egg yolk and leave to rest for 30 minutes.

Bake in an oven at 160 °C for about 15 minutes.

Take them out of the oven and moisten the top of the cakes lightly with water using a brush. Straightaway scatter some pine kernels over the top. Put them back in the oven and let the pine kernels colour slightly.

Leave to cool.

If desired, scatter some icing sugar over the top.

Sponge biscuits

Requirements

250 g butter
250 g icing sugar
5 eggs
300 g plain flour
vanilla essence
piping bag

To make about 50 biscuits

METHOD OF PREPARATION

Butter a baking tray and sieve a little flour over it, or use a non-stick mat.

Preheat the oven to 150 °C.

Beat the butter till light and airy. Add the sugar.

Next add the eggs one by one.

Fold in the sieved flour and the vanilla without allowing more air in.

Pipe little balls, using a piping bag with a smooth nozzle of about 5 mm diameter.

Bake for 10 minutes until they are pale brown at the edges.

If the biscuits have been baked on a baking tray, they will have to be loosened from the tray straightaway.

When they are cool, finish them off by dipping them in precrystallized chocolate.

Allow the chocolate to harden before serving them.

04 milkshakes & chocolate milk

Chocolate ice-cream shake

Requirements

To serve 4 people

500 g chocolate ice-cream
500 g milk
125 g Grand Marnier
blender

METHOD OF PREPARATION

Put the ice-cream and the Grand Marnier in a blender.

Mix until the mixture is completely smooth. Pour it at once into cooled wine glasses and finish off with a garnish.

In the photograph a chocolate spiral has been added. You can find out how to make it on p. 20: 'Quick and easy ways to make cake decorations'.

Copacabana milkshake

Requirements

To serve 4 people

100 g milk
50 g chocolate
80 g demerara sugar
1 1/2 bananas
200 g milk
500 g ice cream
ground cinnamon
blender

METHOD OF PREPARATION

Bring 100 g milk to the boil with the demerara sugar.

Add the chocolate and the ground cinnamon.

Leave this to cool completely.

Chop the banana into pieces and put it with the completely cooled down chocolate drink, the 200 g cold milk and the ice cream in an electric blender.

Mix until it foams. Serve at once in cooled glasses. Scatter a little cinnamon on the foam and place a slice of banana on the rim.

Brazilian chocolate drink

Requirements

To serve 4 people

125 g chocolate
1 cup strong coffee
3 cups of milk
4 tablespoons whipped
cream
20 g sugar

METHOD OF PREPARATION

Finely chop the chocolate.
Make coffee. Bring the milk with the sugar to the boil and pour this on the
chocolate, together with the coffee.
Pour the chocolate milk into cups.
Carefully top each cup with a tablespoon of whipped cream without stirring,
as a garnish.

Mexican chocolate drink

Requirements

To serve 6 people

1500 g milk
110 g sugar
2 sachets vanilla sugar
100 g chocolate
5 g ground cardamom
2 eggs
100 g whipping cream

METHOD OF PREPARATION

Beat the cream lightly to a soft, liquid consistency.

Heat the milk with the sugar, vanilla sugar, cardamom and chocolate.

Meanwhile beat the eggs till light.

Pour some chocolate milk onto the eggs and mix well. Add the egg mixture to the rest of the milk and stir briskly while the whole mixture continues to heat. Don't allow the mixture to boil!

Divide it over six glasses.

Use the whipped cream to garnish and serve at once.

Tropical dream
Crème brûlée with chocolate
Chocolate caramel ice cream
Chocolate and orange mousse
Mocca mousse
Chocolate sabayon
Coffee mousse
Chocolate mousse
Chocolate cake with orange advocaat
Light and airy cake
Pound cake
Chocolate fruit cake
Grandmother's cake with a chocolate ganache
Chocolate honey muffins (American style)
Chocolate bread pudding
Tartlets with raspberry cream
Cheese dessert
White-chocolate bavarois

Mousse with vanilla bavarois
Honey tartlets
Chocolate cream cake
Chocolate ring
Small chocolate rolls
Moelleux with chocolate
Chocolate tubs with chocolate cream
White and dark
Sponge rolls with chocolate cream
Pear cake with chocolate sauce
Lavender cones
Rum cream with orange tuiles
Custard-filled crêpes with chocolate sauce
Chocolate soufflé ice
Chocolate parfait
Chocolate soufflé
Chocolate sandwich spread

05 desserts

Tropical dream

Requirements for the chocolate cream

150 g dark chocolate
250 g cream
250 g Batida de Coco
piping bag

Requirements for the orange custard cream

zest of one orange
250 g milk
250 g cream
50 g sugar
10 g vanilla sugar
3 egg yolks
10 g cornflour
20 g Grand Marnier
sieve
piping bag

To serve 8 people

PREPARING THE CHOCOLATE CREAM

Melt the chocolate.
Add the liqueur and 50 g heated cream to the chocolate.
Beat the rest of the cream until it has thickened, but can still be poured.
Add this to the chocolate mixture and stir gently to a homogeneous cream, so don't stir it too hard.
Use a piping bag to divide this over glasses.
Fill the glasses only half full.
To give it a different look, you can tilt the glasses a little before piping the cream into them. Leave the glasses tilted as long as possible, so that the cream has set sufficiently before the custard is piped in.

PREPARING THE ORANGE CUSTARD CREAM

Wash the orange well and grate the zest off the peel.
Add this grated zest to the milk and cream.
Bring them to the boil and leave to infuse for 30 minutes.
Mix in the egg yolks, the sugars and the cornflour.
Bring the milk and cream back to the boil and pour it through a sieve on the egg-yolk mixture.
Add the Grand Marnier.
Leave it all to thicken on a low heat.
Allow it to become lukewarm and pipe it onto the chocolate cream.
Leave for at least 1 hour in the refrigerator before serving.

Crème brûlée with chocolate

Requirements for the chocolate base

To serve 4 people

METHOD OF PREPARATION

150 g chocolate

150 g cream

50 g sugar

50 g butter

Melt the chocolate.

Bring the cream to the boil with the sugar. Pour this on the chocolate and mix.

Add the soft butter and mix it all to a homogeneous cream.

Divide this over four ovenproof dishes and place these in the refrigerator until the chocolate has lightly set.

Requirements for the custard

4 egg yolks

50 g sugar

250 g cream

2 vanilla pods

Cut the vanilla pods along the length, take out the seeds and add these to the egg yolks.

Whisk the egg yolks with the sugar until frothy.

Add the cream and continue to whisk until it thickens slightly.

Pour this custard on top of the chocolate layer in each dish.

Leave to cook gently in a low oven at about 80 °C.

Requirements for the finish

demerara sugar

Scatter some demerara sugar over the top and place the dishes for a few minutes under the grill, so the sugar on top becomes lightly caramelized.

Serve at once.

Tip: instead of vanilla you can also use dried lavender florets. In that case you have to leave them to infuse in 50 g boiling water for 15 minutes.

Sieve and add the infusion to the custard.

Chocolate caramel ice cream

Requirements

To serve 6 people

400 g full-cream milk
400 g cream
20 g coarsely ground coffee
1 vanilla pod
100 g sugar
120 g chopped chocolate
5 egg yolks
100 g sugar
ice-cream machine

METHOD OF PREPARATION

Bring the milk and the cream to the boil with the coffee and the vanilla pod, which has been cut through lengthwise.

Leave to infuse for 10 minutes.

Pour the milk through a sieve and bring it back to the boil.

Melt 100 g sugar without adding any moisture in a deep saucepan until it has a light-brown colour; stir it with a long wooden spoon until all the sugar has melted.

Take great care, because caramel sugar has a temperature of at least 160 °C.

Very slowly, a little at a time, add the milk to the boiling sugar, while stirring well.

When it has all been stirred in and there are no more lumps, add the chopped chocolate.

Beat the egg yolks with 100 g sugar and slowly add the chocolate mixture to it so that it all heats up gently.

Continue to stir well until the mixture begins to thicken. Don't let it boil.

Leave it to cool completely and then process it in the ice-cream maker.

Chocolate and orange mousse

Requirements

To serve 8 people

180 g chocolate
20 g butter
peel of an orange
3 egg yolks
3 egg whites
30 g Grand Marnier
250 g whipping cream
piping bag

PREPARATORY WORK

First pipe a grid of chocolate (see: Quick and easy ways of making cake decorations, p. 20).
Break this into portions when it has hardened.
Spread a little chocolate on paper and stick pieces of the grid on the still liquid chocolate. They will serve as bases for the dessert.

METHOD OF PREPARATION

Melt the chocolate.
Pull eight long, thin strips from the orange peel with a decorating parer and roll them into small spirals.
Grate the rest of the peel finely. Stir the butter and the grated peel through the chocolate, add the egg yolks and finally the liqueur. Beat the egg whites to soft peaks and carefully fold them into the mixture. Stir it as little as possible so that you don't lose the lightness in it.
Whip the cream to soft peaks and fold it into the mixture. Don't stir it but fold it in carefully. Using a piping bag with a serrated nozzle, pipe the mousse onto the bases and put them in the refrigerator for at least 1 hour. Place the orange spirals on top of the mousse as a decoration, and serve.

Mocca mousse

Requirements

To serve 4 people

100 g chocolate

3 tablespoons milk

50 g butter

1 cup strong coffee (about
200 ml)

1 tablespoon rum

3 eggs

100 g sugar

1/2 teaspoon cinnamon

METHOD OF PREPARATION

Melt the chocolate and add the milk, the rum and the coffee. Stir it all, together with the butter which has been softened, to a smooth cream. Separate the egg yolks and whisk them well with the sugar and the cinnamon. Beat the egg whites to a firm froth. Add the chocolate mixture to the froth. Don't stir, otherwise the cream will become too heavy. You should use a rubber spatula to pull up the froth and the chocolate cream gently until it has all been mixed properly. Put the mousse into glass coupes and place them in the refrigerator for at least 2 hours.

Chocolate sabayon

Requirements

To serve 6 people

200 g dark chocolate
100 g water
1 sachet mint tea
100 g milk
100 g sugar
4 egg yolks
25 g brandy

METHOD OF PREPARATION

Melt the chocolate.

Bring the water to the boil and let the tea infuse for 5 minutes.

Bring the milk to the boil. Beat the egg yolks with the sugar until light and airy.

Pour the milk and the tea a little at a time into the beaten egg yolks and heat it gently on a low heat. Stir well to avoid burning.

Add the chocolate and the brandy and while stirring continuously, bring the cream almost to boiling point.

Put a ball of vanilla ice-cream into a dessert glass.

Pour the warm sabayon over it and serve at once.

Coffee mousse

Requirements

250 g chocolate
200 g espresso coffee
250 g whipping cream
2 sachets of vanilla sugar
piping bag

To serve 6 people

METHOD OF PREPARATION

Melt the chocolate and add the warm coffee to it. Stir to a smooth cream.
Leave to cool.
Beat the cream with the vanilla sugar to a soft peak and mix it into the cooled chocolate cream.
Divide over 6 glasses or fill a large bowl.
If you want to garnish it you can add a few touches of whipped cream or a piece of chocolate.

Chocolate mousse

Requirements

To serve 4 people

100 g chocolate
120 g butter
4 eggs
125 g sugar
a pinch of salt (optional)
plastic film

METHOD OF PREPARATION

Melt the chocolate.

Mix the soft butter and the chocolate to a smooth cream.

Break the eggs and separate the egg whites and the yolks.

Stir the egg yolks smooth and mix them with the chocolate cream.

Whisk the egg whites and the sugar to a firm froth.

Fold the froth very carefully into the mixture without stirring, but by pulling it up gently with a spatula (see also in 'Mocca mousse', p. 87).

Divide it over glasses or make some chocolate tubs, as in the photograph.

Leave to cool before serving.

TO MAKE THE CHOCOLATE TUBS

Cut strips of plastic film 5 cm wide by 20 cm long. Put them flat on the work surface. Spread a thin layer of chocolate on each strip. Wait a moment until the chocolate begins to thicken. Roll each strip into a cylinder. Leave it to harden properly before removing the plastic film.

Chocolate cake with orange advocaat

Requirements for the chocolate cake

3 eggs
125 g icing sugar
75 g plain flour
25 g cornflour
3 tablespoons cocoa
mixer
round cake tin
spatula

Requirements for the orange advocaat

4 egg yolks
150 g sugar
2 sachets vanilla sugar
200 g condensed milk
100 g Cointreau
25 g pure alcohol (ethanol min. 90%, available from licensed stores or pharmacies)
food processor

PREPARATORY WORK

Butter a round cake tin and lightly powder it with flour, so that the cake will turn out easily after baking.
Preheat the oven to 190 °C.
Sift the flour and the cornflour together with the cocoa.

PREPARATION OF THE CHOCOLATE CAKE

Beat the eggs and the sugar in a bowl with a mixer to a thick, but light mousse.
Slowly add the sifted flour mixture to the batter and mix carefully, without stirring too hard. Use a spatula or pan scraper for this.
Pour the mixture into the buttered and floured cake tin and bake it for about 40 minutes in the oven until the cake feels springy in the middle.
Turn out onto a rack to cool.

PREPARATION OF THE ORANGE ADVOCAAT

Mix the sugar with the vanilla sugar and the egg yolks in a food processor.
Slowly add the milk, the liqueur and the alcohol.
Mix for at least 1 minute at the highest speed.
Pour the drink at once into a bottle and close it.
In this way the advocaat will keep for at least a year.

TO FINISH

Before serving, dribble the orange advocaat generously over the cake.

Light and airy cake

Requirements

To make about 2 cakes

100 g butter
150 g sugar
3 eggs
125 g chocolate
100 g plain flour
1/2 sachet of baking powder
piping bag

METHOD OF PREPARATION

Butter the cake tins and powder them with a thin covering of flour or use a non-stick tin. Preheat the over to 190 °C.

Mix the butter with the sugar and the egg yolks and stir them well to a creamy consistency.

Sift the flour and the baking powder and mix them carefully through the butter mixture.

Melt the chocolate and add this to the mixture.

Whisk the egg whites to firm peaks and fold them carefully through the mixture. Don't stir it, but fold it in to keep a light dough.

With a piping bag, pipe long strips of this mixture into the tins.

Put them in the oven for about 45 minutes.

Place the cakes on a rack to cool after baking.

Pound cake

Requirements

For 2 cake tins about 22 cm long

250 g butter

250 g sugar

5 eggs

250 g plain flour

1/2 sachet of baking powder
(optional)

150 g chocolate bar

METHOD OF PREPARATION

Chop the chocolate into small pieces. Butter the two cake tins or use non-stick tins.
Stir the butter till light and airy. Beat the eggs with the sugar till light and stir this
into the butter. Mix the flour and the baking powder into the mixture and finally
add the chocolate chips. Bake in an oven at 200 to 210 °C for about 45 minutes.
To test if the cake has baked for long enough, prick it in the middle with a knife.
The knife should be dry when it is pulled out.

Chocolate fruit cake

Requirements for the cake

175 g soft butter
100 g sugar
50 g honey
4 eggs
110 g chocolate
50 g raisins
25 g chopped walnuts
peel of half an orange
225 g plain flour
10 g baking powder
1 tablespoon lemon juice
mixed spices (optional)

Requirements for the icing

250 g sugar
100 g milk
30 g butter (optional)

To fill a cake tin about 25 cm long

PREPARING THE CAKE

Preheat the oven to 170 °C. Butter a cake tin or use a non-stick tin.
Chop the orange peel very finely. Chop the raisins, the walnuts and the chocolate finely. Beat the butter and sugar till light and add the honey. Add the eggs one by one. Add the baking powder (and the mixed spice) to the flour. Mix the orange peel, the lemon juice, the chopped nuts and raisins and the chopped chocolate into the flour and then into the butter mixture. Mix well. Put the batter into the tin and press a dip into the middle with a spoon. Bake for 60 minutes. After baking, allow it to cool to lukewarm before turning it out of the tin. If desired, glaze the cake with the sugar icing.

PREPARING THE ICING

Bring the milk, the sugar (and the butter if used) to the boil while stirring with a wooden spoon. Take the spoon out of the pan and continue to heat to 112 - 115 °C without stirring. If you have no thermometer to measure the temperature, then take a small bowl with cold water. Drop a little of the syrup into it from the wooden spoon. Wait a moment to make sure that the syrup sample is quite cold. If the syrup forms a small ball in the water, the correct temperature will have been reached. Simply leave the syrup to cool (still without stirring). As soon as the syrup is lukewarm, stir it briskly until it begins to look thick and milky. Now leave it to cool completely. The icing will have firmed up on the surface but will become soft and creamy again in use. Keep the icing in a firmly closed bowl. Every time you need a glaze, you can put the desired quantity in a small pan and make it lukewarm (about 35 °C) while stirring. Pour the icing over the cake.

Grandmother's cake with a chocolate ganache

Requirements for the cake

To make 1 cake (6 people)

100 g butter

150 g sugar

100 g egg yolks

70 g egg whites

80 g plain flour

40 g cornflour

2 g baking powder

spatula

PREPARING GRANDMOTHER'S CAKE

Preheat the oven to 180 to 190 °C.

Beat the butter together with 1/3 of the sugar and the egg yolks till frothy.

Beat the egg whites with the rest of the sugar till it forms firm peaks.

Fold this into the butter mixture with a spatula.

Sift the flour with the cornflour and the baking powder and fold this carefully into the butter mixture.

Bake for 40 to 50 minutes.

Turn out the cake and leave it to cool on a rack.

Requirements for the ganache

150 g cream

30 g sugar

210 g dark chocolate

30 g butter

PREPARING THE GANACHE

Chop the chocolate fine.

Bring the cream with the sugar to the boil and pour this at once onto the chopped chocolate. Mix well. Add the butter to the mixture and stir till quite smooth. Place the rack with the cake on a baking sheet and pour the ganache generously over it. Move the rack about a little so that the ganache spreads evenly over it.

Chocolate honey muffins (American style)

Requirements

To serve 14 people

450 g plain flour
15 g baking powder
100 g cocoa
400 g butter
350 g icing sugar
80 g honey
7 eggs
zest of 1 orange
sieve

METHOD OF PREPARATION

Preheat the oven to 170 °C. Butter fourteen muffin tins about 7 cm diameter, or two traditional cake tins about 25 cm long. Sift the flour together with the baking powder and the cocoa. Beat the butter (which should be at room temperature) with the icing sugar and the honey until light. Add the eggs one by one while beating continuously. Without further beating, mix in the flour and finely chopped orange peel. Pour the mixture into the tins. Bake for about 1 hour and 15 minutes. Leave to cool before turning them out of the tins.

Chocolate bread pudding

Requirements

6 large slices of bread
100 g sugar
1 sachet of vanilla sugar
500 g milk
3 eggs
100 g chocolate
100 g raisins

To serve 4 people

METHOD OF PREPARATION

Butter a mould and dust it with flour or use a non-stick mould.
Preheat the oven to 180 °C.
Cut the bread into cubes of about 1 x 1 cm and put them in a bowl together with the raisins. Beat the eggs with the sugar till frothy. Meanwhile bring the milk to the boil and stir the chopped chocolate into the milk. Pour the chocolate milk onto the egg batter and mix it all. Next pour the whole mixture onto the combined bread and raisins.
Mix everything until all liquid has been absorbed by the bread. Leave to rest for 10 minutes. Pour the mixture into the mould and bake it for about 1 hour and 30 minutes.

Tartlets with raspberry cream

Requirements

100 g milk
100 g cream
50 g raspberries
25 g sugar
3 egg yolks
120 g chocolate
small pastry moulds
brush
piping bag

To make 10 tartlets

SHORT PASTRY

(see p. 113)

METHOD OF PREPARATION

Roll out the short pastry to about 3 mm thickness. Line the pastry moulds with it and prick a few holes in the bottom with the tip of a knife. Leave to rest for 20 minutes. Bake in an oven at 160 °C for 15 minutes.

FILLING

Melt the chocolate
Puree the raspberries.
Bring the milk, the cream and the sugar to the boil. Add the raspberry puree and then the egg yolks. Allow to thicken on a low heat while stirring well. Meanwhile beat the cream to soft peaks and fold it into the melted chocolate. Pour the boiled mixture onto the melted chocolate and leave it to cool. Using a brush, spread a thin film of chocolate inside the tartlets. Leave to set. Using a piping bag with a smooth nozzle, pipe a small mound of the raspberry cream into the tartlets.
Add a garnish.

Cheese dessert

Requirements

To serve 4 people

250 g sugar

100 g water

250 g goat's cheese

6 egg yolks

Amaretto liqueur

Heatproof dishes or use

cup-shaped orange tuiles

METHOD OF PREPARATION

Bring the sugar and water to the boil.

Meanwhile stir the cheese till smooth.

Add the boiled sugar and water to the cheese and stir until you have a smooth mixture.

If necessary, pour it through a sieve.

Beat the egg yolks till light and airy and stir them through the cheese mixture.

Heat all this until the mixture begins to thicken.

Add the melted chocolate.

Flavour to taste with Amaretto liqueur.

Pour the mixture into heatproof dishes or orange tuiles (see 'Rum cream with orange tuiles', p. 133. As soon as the tuiles come out of the oven, bend the edges quickly upwards to form dishes.)

If using heatproof dishes, put them briefly under the grill to allow the surface to brown slightly, or if there is no grill, place them in an oven at 220 °C for a few minutes until the surface turns light brown. Obviously, if you are using orange tuiles you can't heat them up again.

White-chocolate bavarois

Requirements for the white-chocolate bavarois

135 g full-cream milk
65 g egg yolks
40 g sugar
1 vanilla pod
5 g gelatine
120 g white chocolate
380 g partly whipped cream
spatula
8 small pudding moulds

Requirements for the port ganache

100 g chocolate
50 g cream
50 g port

To serve 8 people

PREPARATION OF THE WHITE-CHOCOLATE BAVAROIS

Soak the gelatine in cold water.

Chop the chocolate finely.

Heat the milk, the sugar, the vanilla pod which has been cut in half lengthwise, and the egg yolks until they thicken slightly. Remove the vanilla pod.

Squeeze the water out of the soaked gelatine leaves and add them to the chopped chocolate. Stir to a smooth cream.

Leave this mixture to cool to about 30 °C.

Beat the cream to a soft peak.

Fold the cream into the chocolate mixture with a spatula.

Pour the mixture into small moulds and leave them in the refrigerator to set for two to three hours.

Before serving, briefly dip the bottom of each mould in warm water and turn it out onto a pretty dessert plate.

Finish off with a garnish.

If desired serve a port ganache with it.

PREPARING THE PORT GANACHE

Melt the chocolate.

Stir the port into it and then the cream which should be at room temperature.

Mousse with vanilla bavarois

Requirements for the sponge base

1 egg
3 egg yolks
50 g sugar
20 g plain flour
10 g ground almonds
non-stick foil

Requirements for the bavarois

250 g milk
1 vanilla pod
3 egg yolks
60 g sugar
50 g white chocolate
2 1/2 gelatine leaves

Requirements for the dark mousse

150 g dark chocolate
65 g full-cream milk
200 g whipping cream

To serve about 15 people

PREPARING THE SPONGE BASE

Preheat the oven to 180 °C. Cover a baking tray of about 30 x 40 cm with non-stick foil. Beat the egg with the egg yolks and the sugar till light and airy. Sift the flour with the ground almonds and mix it into the egg froth. Pour it onto the baking tray. Bake for about 15 minutes.

PREPARING THE BAVAROIS

Soak the gelatine in cold water. Cut a vanilla pod lengthwise and scrape the soft seeds out of it. Bring the milk with the vanilla seeds and pod to the boil. Remove the pod. Mix the egg yolks with the sugar. Pour the boiling milk slowly onto the egg yolks while stirring well, and continue to heat to boiling point. Add the white chocolate and let it cool down to lukewarm. Wring the excess water out of the gelatine and add the gelatine to the mixture. Beat the cream to a soft peak and fold it into the mixture.

PREPARING THE DARK MOUSSE

Melt the chocolate. Heat the milk to about 30 °C and stir it into the chocolate. Whip the cream to a soft peak and fold it into the chocolate mixture.

TO FINISH

Take the sponge from the baking foil and put it on a plate with a raised edge. If you don't have the right size, you can distribute the sponge over two rectangular ovenproof dishes. Spread the bavarois evenly over the cooled-down sponge.
Place in the refrigerator for 30 minutes. Make the dark mousse and spread this evenly over the set bavarois. Leave to cool for a few hours before serving. Before cutting it, dip the knife briefly in hot water. If desired, decorate the top with a garnish.

Honey tartlets

Requirements for short-crust pastry for the tartlets

250 g butter
250 g icing sugar
3 eggs
500 g plain flour
10 g baking powder
vanilla, lemon or cinnamon
for flavouring

Requirements for the honey ganache

200 g whipping cream
40 g butter
50 g lavender honey
(or honey + 1 g lavender powder*)
250 g chocolate (pure, milk or white)

To serve about 8 people

PREPARING THE TARTLETS

Preheat the oven to 180 °C.
Sift the flour and the baking powder.
Soften the butter and mix it with the icing sugar.
Add the eggs one by one and then the flour and the flavouring.
Mix all ingredients to a smooth mixture. Don't mix it for longer than necessary.
Cover and leave to rest in the refrigerator for 30 minutes.
Roll out the dough to an even thickness. Use a little flour to avoid the dough sticking to the working surface.
Line tartlet moulds with dough. With the tip of a knife prick a few holes in the base to avoid it rising up.
Bake for 12 minutes.

PREPARING THE HONEY GANACHE

Chop the chocolate finely.
Bring the cream with the butter (and if used the lavender powder) to the boil.
Pour the mixture onto the chocolate and stir until the chocolate has melted; add the honey and stir to a smooth cream.
Distribute the cream over the pastry tartlets.
Place them into the refrigerator for at least 1 hour.

* Dried lavender is available in supermarkets.
You can make lavender powder by crushing dried lavender fine in a hand blender.

Chocolate cream cake

Requirements for the cake base

225 g plain flour
30 g cocoa
150 g butter
30 g sugar
20 g cold milk
sieve

Requirements for the filling

175 g butter
300 g brown sugar candy
50 g honey
4 eggs
50 g cocoa
150 g dark chocolate
300 g cream
50 g plain flour
chocolate flakes

To serve about 10 people

PREPARING THE CAKE BASE (APPROX. 30 CM IN DIAMETER)

Sift the flour and cocoa into a bowl.
Stir in the soft butter in bits. Add the milk and sugar and mix well until you have a smooth mixture.
Roll out the dough on a floured working surface to a slab the size of the cake tin (about 30 cm diameter).
Leave the dough to rest for 1 hour.

PREPARING THE FILLING

Melt the chocolate.
Beat the butter, sugar and honey till light and airy.
Add the cocoa and flour and then the eggs one by one.
Make sure it is light and airy before stirring in the melted chocolate and finally the cream.
Pour this filling over the dough.
Bake in an oven at 170 °C for about 1 hour and 20 minutes.
Leave the cake to cool down completely.
If desired, whip up 400 g cream with a little sugar and completely cover the top of the cake with it.
Scatter some chocolate flakes over the top as a garnish.

Chocolate ring

Requirements

260 g chocolate

100 g butter

8 egg yolks

8 egg whites

60 g sugar

250 g strong, sweetened
coffee

35 boudoir biscuits

spatula

deep ring mould

To serve 8 people

CHOCOLATE SPONGE

Melt the chocolate and add the butter.

Add the egg yolks one by one and mix well.

While this mixture cools down to lukewarm, beat the egg whites with the sugar to a
froth.

First add 1/4 of the froth to the chocolate mixture, then carefully fold in the rest.

Use the spatula to pull the mixture up and don't stir, otherwise it will lose its
lightness.

Take a deep ring mould.

Briefly soak the boudoirs in the strong coffee and then arrange them round the
cake mould, close together, with the bent sides against the tin.

Fill the mould with the chocolate cream. Cover the top of the cream with the
remaining boudoirs.

Cover the ring with a cellophane film to stop it drying out and put it overnight in
the refrigerator.

Turn it out on a pretty dish.

Small chocolate rolls

Requirements

2 egg whites
75 g plain flour
75 g icing sugar
10 g ground almonds
40 g butter
piping bag

Requirements for the filling

200 g dark chocolate
200 g milk chocolate
280 g cream
10 g aniseed
100 g butter
piping bag

To make 15 small rolls

METHOD OF PREPARATION

Butter a baking tray or use a non-stick baking mat
Preheat the oven to 250 °C.
Mix the egg whites with the icing sugar, the flour, the ground almonds and the melted butter. Stir well.
Using a piping bag, pipe fifteen small heaps about 10 cm apart on the baking tray, or use 2 teaspoons to make fifteen small heaps of equal size on the baking tray.
Bake for about 5 minutes.
Take the biscuits out of the oven as soon as they begin to colour at the edges, and roll them at once one after the other round a thick pencil.
Leave them to cool.

PREPARING THE FILLING

Bring the cream with the aniseed to the boil. Take it off the heat to infuse until the cream has cooled to room temperature. Melt the chocolate.
Pour the cream through a sieve and then mix it with the melted chocolate.
Finally mix in the butter, which should be at room temperature, until you have a smooth mixture. Pipe the filling into the rolls with a piping bag.

TO FINISH

If desired, dip both ends into pre-crystallized chocolate when the filling has set.

Moelleux with chocolate

Requirements

To serve 8 people

4 eggs

200 g sugar

50 g brown sugar

40 g honey

140 g chocolate

125 g plain flour

200 g cream

cake mould with a raised

rim of about 3 to 4 cm

METHOD OF PREPARATION

Melt the chocolate or grate the chocolate finely.

Butter a cake mould with an upright edge of about 3 to 4 cm, and scatter a little
flour into it.

Beat the eggs with both sugars and the honey till light and airy.

Add the chocolate, then the flour and finally the partly whipped cream.

Pour the mixture into the mould and bake at 190 °C for about 40 minutes.

Leave to cool before turning out.

Chocolate tubs with chocolate cream

Requirements

2 egg yolks

75 g butter

25 g icing sugar

150 g cream

50 g milk

70 g grenadine

150 g dark chocolate

a little liqueur (optional)

4 small balloons

greaseproof paper

foil

piping bag

To make 4 tubs

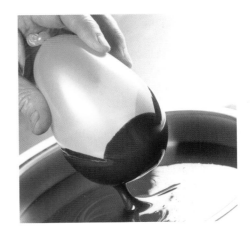

PREPARATION OF THE TUBS

Blow up the balloons and knot them to close.

Dip them for about 1/3 into pre-crystallized chocolate and place them carefully upright on greaseproof paper or aluminium foil.

Put them in the refrigerator as soon as the chocolate begins to set.

After 10 minutes remove the balloons by pricking them with a pointed knife.

PREPARATION OF THE CHOCOLATE CREAM

Melt the chocolate.

Whisk the cream to a soft peak.

Mix the sugar with the egg yolks, stir in the butter which should be at room temperature. Stir until smooth.

Add the chocolate and then the milk, the grenadine and, if desired, a little liqueur.

Mix the soft whipped cream into the chocolate mixture. Immediately pipe the mixture into the chocolate tubs, using a piping bag with a serrated nozzle.

Place in the refrigerator for 1 hour before serving.

White and dark

Requirements for the chocolate sponge

50 g egg yolks

125 g eggs

100 g sugar

80 g egg whites

40 g sugar

30 g plain flour

30 g cocoa

sieve

Requirements for the dark chocolate mousse

150 g dark chocolate

65 g milk

200 g whipping cream

Requirements for the white chocolate mousse

75 g milk

20 g vanilla sugar

23 g egg yolks

3 g custard powder

1/2 leaf of gelatine

150 g white chocolate

340 g whipping cream

palette knife

To serve 16 people

PREPARING THE CHOCOLATE SPONGE

Sift the flour with the cocoa. Beat the eggs and the egg yolks together with 100 g sugar until light and airy. Beat the egg whites to a firm peak with 40 g sugar.

Carefully fold in first the egg whites into the egg yolks and then the flour. Don't stir too much. Spread this mixture thinly on a non-stick baking foil on two baking trays of about 30 x 20 cm. Bake for 10 minutes at 220 °C.

PREPARING THE DARK CHOCOLATE MOUSSE

Melt the chocolate. Heat the milk to about 40 °C and add the chocolate. Whip the cream to soft peaks and mix it with the chocolate cream.

PREPARING THE WHITE CHOCOLATE MOUSSE

Chop the chocolate finely. Soak the gelatine in cold water.

Make a custard with the milk, sugar, egg yolks and custard powder. Add the squeezed out gelatine to it and pour this onto the chocolate. Mix well. Leave to cool to below 30 °C. Finally add the lightly whipped cream.

FINISHING OFF THE CAKE

Spread the dark chocolate mousse evenly on one of the sponge bases. Stick the second sponge base on top of the mousse. Leave to set in the refrigerator. Spread the white chocolate mousse evenly over the second sponge layer. Pat the surface with a palette knife to create a relief to decorate the top. Leave to set in the refrigerator before dividing into squares. Garnish as you wish.

Sponge rolls with chocolate cream

Requirements for the sponge

4 eggs
3 egg yolks
140 g sugar
90 g plain flour

Requirements for the chocolate cream

400 g chocolate
600 g cream
100 g butter

To serve 10 people (2 rolls)

PREPARING THE SPONGE CAKE

Cover two baking trays of about 30 x 40 cm with a non-stick baking mat. The eggs and the egg yolks, together with the sugar, are first beaten warm and then cold: in other words, place the bowl with the egg mixture in a bain marie and beat the mixture briskly until it is lukewarm. You then remove the bowl from the hot water and continue to beat until the mixture is completely cold. If you use a blender or mixer you can apply heat by using a hairdryer round the outside of the mixing bowl. Mix the sifted flour carefully with the beaten egg, without stirring but by gently moving the spatula up through the froth. Take care not to mix it more than is necessary. Spread the mixture evenly over the baking trays. Bake in an oven at 190 to 200 °C for 10 minutes.
Immediately after baking, cut the edge loose and turn the baking tray over onto a tea towel or on greaseproof paper.

PREPARING THE CHOCOLATE CREAM

Bring 100 g cream to the boil and melt the chocolate. Pour the cream over the chocolate and stir it until you have a homogeneous mixture. Bring this to room temperature and add the butter. Leave the chocolate mixture to cool down completely. Beat the rest of the cream to a soft peak and mix it with the chocolate mixture. Remove the non-stick foil from the baked sponge. If the edges are dry and crumbly, cut them off with a knife. Spread 2/3 of the chocolate cream onto the sponge. Roll the slabs carefully to a cylinder and put the end of it underneath. Spread the remaining cream on the outside. You can give it a finishing touch with some chocolate flakes. Place the rolls in the refrigerator for at least 1 hour before cutting and serving them.

Pear cake with chocolate sauce

Requirements for the cake

100 g plain flour
30 g ground almonds
60 g butter
60 g milk

Requirements for the filling

400 g halved pears in syrup
(bottled or tinned)
50 g butter
50 g sugar
2 eggs
100 g ground almonds
15 g cocoa

*Requirements for the chocolate
sauce*

90 g chocolate
50 g milk
20 g butter

To serve 6 people

TO PREPARE THE PEAR CAKE
Butter a cake tin.
Mix the flour with the ground almonds and knead the butter into it until the dough
becomes 'crumbly'.
Add the milk so that the dough softens.
Cover the dough and leave it to rest for 15 minutes in the refrigerator.
Roll out the dough evenly and line the cake tin with it. Use the tip of a knife to prick
holes in the bottom, to avoid blisters forming.
Preheat the oven to 200 °C.
Allow the pears to drain. Meanwhile beat the sugar with the butter till light and
airy, add the eggs one by one, and finally add the cocoa and the ground almonds.
Distribute this mixture over the cake base. Distribute the pears over the surface
with the rounded side up, and push them gently into the soft mixture.
Bake for about 30 minutes.
Leave to cool down and scatter with a little icing sugar.

TO PREPARE THE CHOCOLATE SAUCE
Bring the butter to room temperature.
Melt the chocolate and add the warmed milk to it.
Finally stir the butter through the sauce.

Cut the cake into portions and serve each piece with a little chocolate sauce on the
side of the plate.

Lavender cones

Requirements for the cones

50 g butter
100 g icing sugar
60 g plain flour
2 egg whites
piping bag

Requirements for the filling

200 g milk chocolate
100 g milk
ground lavender powder
300 g cream
piping bag

To make 12 cones

PREPARING THE CONES

Butter a baking tray or use a non-stick baking mat.

Grind the dried lavender to a powder in a food processor.

Preheat the oven to 150 °C.

Beat the butter creamy. Add the sugar. Mix in first half the egg white, then the flour, and finally the remainder of the egg white. Cover and leave to set in the refrigerator for 1 hour.

Using a piping bag, pipe twelve small heaps onto the baking tray about 10 cm apart, or use two teaspoons to make the small mounds.

Bake for about 12 minutes. As soon as the biscuits begin to colour at the edge, take them out of the oven and shape them into cones straightaway.

Leave them to cool.

PREPARING THE FILLING

Melt the chocolate, bring the milk to the boil with the lavender and stir it with the chocolate to a smooth mixture. Leave to cool. Beat the cream and stir it through the chocolate mixture.

Use a piping bag to pipe the filling into the cones.

Rum cream with orange tuiles

Requirements for the tuiles

zest of 1 orange peel
100 g icing sugar
15 g plain flour
20 g orange juice
100 g almonds
80 g butter

*Requirements for the rum
cream*

225 g chocolate
4 egg yolks
4 egg whites
75 g sugar
60 g brown rum
60 g cream
spatula
piping bag

To make 40 tuiles

PREPARING THE ORANGE TUILES

Preheat the oven to 150 °C.
Wash and dry the peel of the orange very well and grate the orange zest.
Avoid the white part of the peel, as it gives a bitter taste.
Chop the almonds finely.
Mix the zest, the sugar, the flour, the chopped almonds and the orange juice.
Next add the butter, which should be melted.
Leave to rest in the refrigerator for 1 hour.
Scoop half teaspoons of the mixture and shape them into small balls.
Put them on a non-stick baking tray, at least 10 cm apart.
Push the balls flat; try to keep a round shape.
Make sure the little balls are not too large, because the dough spreads considerably during baking.
Bake for about 15 minutes, until the tuiles are slightly coloured.
Leave them to cool down partly, before removing them from the baking tray.
Keep the tuiles in a closed container.

To serve 8 people

PREPARING THE RUM CREAM

Melt the chocolate. Beat the yolks with the sugar until it is frothy and the colour turns pale. Add the rum and then the chocolate. Beat the egg whites briskly to firm peaks. Gently fold first 1/4 of the egg white into the batter with the spatula, without stirring, and then the remainder. Mix well, but no longer than necessary. Pipe a large rosette on a small plate or dish and put it in the refrigerator for at least 1 hour. Put the tuiles alongside the cream by way of decoration.

Custard-filled crêpes with chocolate sauce

Requirements for the crêpes

For 6 people

250 g plain flour
500 g milk
5 eggs
25 g sugar
a pinch of salt
1 tablespoon oil or a little
melted butter

PREPARING THE CRÊPES

Add the sugar, salt and the oil or melted butter to the flour.
Beat the eggs till light and airy and add them to the flour mixture. Add a little milk and beat it until you have a thick, smooth batter without lumps. Slowly add the rest of the milk. Leave the batter to rest for 30 minutes. If the batter is too thick, add a little more milk. For thin crêpes it has to be fairly runny. Melt a little butter in a hot frying pan, pour a little batter into it and cook the crêpes till they are golden brown. Pile the crêpes onto a plate.

Requirements for the vanilla custard

500 g milk
50 g sugar
25 g cornflour
1 sachet vanilla sugar

PREPARING THE VANILLA CUSTARD

Take 1/3 of the cold milk and dissolve the cornflour into it until there are no lumps left in it. Bring the remaining milk to the boil with the sugar. Add the cold cornflour mixture to the boiling milk and whisk it well. Leave to simmer for a moment and take it off the heat.

Requirements for the chocolate sauce

300 g chocolate
200 g cream

PREPARING THE CHOCOLATE SAUCE

Chop the chocolate finely. Bring the cream to the boil and pour it onto the chocolate pieces. Stir well until you have a homogeneous sauce.

TO FINISH

Put vanilla custard into the middle of each crêpe.
Roll up the crêpes and arrange them on a serving dish.
Just before serving pour the hot chocolate sauce over them.

Chocolate soufflé ice

Requirements

125 g milk
18 g cocoa
3 egg yolks
100 g sugar
75 g chocolate
250 g cream
cellophane

To serve 10 people

METHOD OF PREPARATION

Sift the cocoa. Chop the chocolate finely. Bring the milk to the boil with the cocoa. Beat the egg yolks with the sugar to a froth and slowly add the boiled chocolate milk while beating continuously. Add the chopped chocolate to the hot mixture and stir until it has melted. Leave the mixture to cool to lukewarm. Whip the cream to a half-way stage and mix it carefully through the chocolate mixture. Fill moulds or small bowls with the soufflé and leave it to freeze for a few hours. Finish off with a garnish before serving. To turn out the soufflé, dip the mould first very briefly in hot water and turn it out onto a plate straightaway.

TO GARNISH (SEE PHOTOGRAPH)

Cut a triangle out of thin cellophane.
Put the cellophane flat on the table and spread it very thinly with precrystallized chocolate. Leave to harden slightly and then wrap it round the frozen soufflé.

Chocolate parfait

Requirements

To serve 5 people

150 g chocolate
125 g butter
100 g sweetened condensed
milk
4 eggs
50 g Cointreau
40 g orange juice
chocolate flakes

METHOD OF PREPARATION

Melt the chocolate.

Beat the butter with the sweetened condensed milk to a smooth cream. Add the egg yolks, the orange juice and the Cointreau and finally the chocolate. Whisk the egg whites to a froth and mix this into the batter. Pour the mixture into a buttered mould and place it in the freezing compartment for 12 hours. Dip the mould very briefly in hot water and turn it out onto a previously chilled dish.

If desired, garnish with a few chocolate flakes and serve immediately.

Chocolate soufflé

Requirements

To serve 4 people

100 g dark chocolate
60 g butter
25 g cocoa
2 egg yolks
4 egg whites
25 g sugar
4 ovenproof dishes
spatula
sieve

METHOD OF PREPARATION

Preheat the oven to 200 °C.

Melt the chocolate in a bain marie. Add the butter and stir the mixture until smooth.

Sift the cocoa and stir this into the melted chocolate.

Beat the egg yolks loose and mix them into the chocolate.

Butter four ovenproof dishes and powder the bottom and sides with a little icing sugar.

Whisk the egg whites with the sugar to a firm, but not too solid, froth.

Carefully fold 1/3 of the egg whites into the chocolate mixture, without stirring, but by gently moving the spatula through it. Do the same with the rest of the froth.

Distribute the mixture over the four dishes, powder them with some sifted icing sugar, and bake for 12 minutes.

Serve immediately, if desired with a small ball of vanilla ice cream.

Chocolate sandwich spread

Requirements for the chocolate spread with dark chocolate

150 g dark chocolate
200 g butter
1 tin of about 400 g
sweetened condensed milk
30 g cocoa
sieve

Requirements for the chocolate spread with milk chocolate

200 g milk chocolate
200 g butter
1 tin of about 400 g
sweetened condensed milk

For about 750 to 800 g chocolate spread

METHOD OF PREPARATION

Melt the chocolate and mix it with the butter to a smooth cream.
Add the sweetened milk.
Mix until the spread is quite smooth.
Transfer it straightaway to jars and seal them.
If stored in a cool place, the chocolate spread will stay fresh for at least a month.

Ingredient Register

Acknowledgements

I would like to offer a special word of thanks to my wife for her support and help in creating this recipe book,
Chocolate Without Borders.
Thanks are also due to the firms of Moldart and of Magimix for their generosity in making the material available
for putting the book together, and to Callebaut, the chocolate makers, for their technical support.
For more information about the materials used visit www.moldart.be and www.magimix.com.

JEAN-PIERRE WYBAUW

www.lannoo.com

Lannoo Publishers
Kasteelstraat 97 – B 8700 Tielt
lannoo@lannoo.be
Postbus 1080 – NL 7230 AB Warnsveld
boeken@lannoo.nl

Author: Jean-Pierre Wybauw
Photography: Frank Croes
English translation: Alastair and Cora Weir
Concept and design: Whitespray bvba
Layout: Mediactief bvba

© Lannoo Publishers, Tielt, Belgium, 2006
Printed and bound by Lannoo Printers, Tielt, Belgium, 2006
D/2006/45/423 – NUR 441
ISBN 13: 978-90-209-6819-4
ISBN 10: 90-209-6819-X

All rights reserved.
No part of this publication may be reproduced, stored in an automated database
and/or published in any form or by any means, electronic, mechanical or otherwise,
without prior written permission from the publisher